NATURE SPEAKS

Nature SPEAKS

MAY WE LISTEN

LARISA LAKE

Red Elixir
Rhinebeck, New York

Paperback ISBN 978-1-960090-94-2
eBook ISBN 978-1-960090-95-9

Library of Congress Control Number
2024922670

Book and cover design by Colin Rolfe

Red Elixir is an imprint of Monkfish Book
Publishing Company

Red Elixir
22 East Market Street, Suite 304
Rhinebeck, New York 12572
(845) 876-4861
redelixirbooks.com

CONTENTS

CHAPTER ONE
We Are Nature

CHAPTER TWO
The Balance of Yin and Yang

CHAPTER THREE
Women and Men

CHAPTER FOUR
To Lead Must Follow

CHAPTER FIVE
Not All Men

CHAPTER SIX
It's Not Biology

CHAPTER SEVEN
Hierarchy

CHAPTER EIGHT
Alignment

CHAPTER NINE
Conclusion

Chapter One

WE ARE NATURE

We are nature. We share minerals with the Earth. We are made up of Earth's elements. We are not separate. We are very literally her children. Every living thing on this planet is made up of Earth's elements. If we are all her children, including animals and trees, then we are all siblings. To separate from this knowledge, one separates from self and all others.

Since we are made up of nature's elements, we are nature. To know oneself is to know nature; to know nature is to know oneself. Meditation is the best way to understand self, and therefore all nature. We are not separate.

This is an important concept as we move forward into this book. It is the basic foundation for truth. Truth is the ultimate goal in knowledge.

Chapter Two

THE BALANCE OF
YIN AND YANG

Yin and yang are the foundational principles of Traditional Chinese Medicine. In the first year of training to become a licensed acupuncturist, it is drilled in that all illnesses are essentially caused by an imbalance of yin and yang. Balanced yin and yang equates to good health, whereas an imbalance equals sickness. There is currently a huge imbalance of yin and yang in today's society. Therefore, there is illness.

Firstly, let's discuss what yin and yang are. We will not be discussing the nuances;

this will be a very brief introduction to the concept. We are probably all familiar with the yin/yang symbol. Yin is the color black, yang is the color white, and there are equal amounts of each to form a perfect circle. Yin is the feminine, substance, form, fluids, cold, darkness, and water. Yang is the masculine, movement, heat, light, daytime, and fire.

Everything can be broken down into yin and yang, and even further and further, where within every yin there is yang, and vice versa. This is represented in the yin/yang symbol with the black yin dot within the white yang side, and the yang dot within the black yin side.

As we mentioned above, when there is an imbalance of yin and yang there will be illness. For example, if there is deficient yang, there will be illness, and if there is deficient yin, there will be illness.

In this philosophy, the masculine is attributed to yang and the feminine is attributed to yin. Please note, in regard to the masculine and feminine, we are talking about archetypal energy that both men and women carry.

The imbalance our society is incurring is excess yang and deficient yin. Our culture is masculine-driven and dominated, and therefore the yang is in overdrive. We can see this in the excess of production causing environmental pollution, overworked and fatigued workers, and the cultural obsession with activity and success. These are all yang attributes: movement, productivity, activity.

This excess yang comes at a cost, as it is harming the yin, leading to severe yin deficiency. Earth, at the macro level, is the feminine and yin. Earth is being destroyed in the name of progress. Trees are being cut down and rivers are being polluted. We are destroying the yin, which is the substance of life. The excess yang creates heat and we are seeing how this is harming the cooling yin and leading to global warming.

If we observe animals in nature, we are observing harmonious living. One thing that is apparent, in regard to the difference between wild animals and human society, is that animals rest a lot. Outside of habitat-building and foraging/hunting for food, animals spend a lot of time preening, resting and digesting. They are living in harmony and the yin and yang are naturally balanced.

Animals do not feel the need to produce anything beyond necessity, as they are behaving true to their nature. When one behaves true to one's nature, yin and yang will be balanced and harmonious.

Currently, society is not behaving true to nature, and since we value yang over yin, productivity over rest, activity over stillness, action over inaction, we are making ourselves sick.

If we were true to our nature, we would rest more. This rest would benefit us both individually and as a society, but, most importantly, Earth would have a chance to heal. The yang activities are harming the yin matter, hence excess yang and deficient yin leading to disharmony, as we are not currently living in alignment with nature.

Chapter Three

WOMEN AND MEN

Women and men are more alike than different. Culture and learned behavior play the biggest part in the differentiation. Both men and women carry yin and yang, which means both men and women carry feminine and masculine. Feminine and masculine are taught, as gender and gender roles are not biology and, in fact, due to socialization starting at a young age.

We live in a male-dominated culture, therefore the masculine (and men) are exalted. Sadly, in the exaltation of the masculine, the feminine has become devalued and synonymous with weakness and other qualities deemed unworthy. This is to the extent that a man being likened to a woman is an insult.

As said earlier, every human carries both yin (feminine) and yang (masculine), therefore society pressuring men to deny their yin is creating a population of men that are denying a part of themselves. To be true to one's nature, one has to accept and allow all parts of oneself, otherwise one becomes lopsided. In this case, it is excess yang and deficient yin. The shame and self-denial a man may carry around his own feminine energies cause him to project negativity upon those that display the feminine externally. This has created a culture where women are seen as less-than and are demeaned.

The belief that the feminine is weak is impacting the yin and yang balance. This is clearly a wrong belief, since most, if not all, feminine qualities are due to an internal strength. One such trait is gentleness. To be gentle requires deep inner resilience and trust in oneself. The harder and edgier someone appears, the deeper the feeling of internal vulnerability. If one feels true self-confidence in themselves, one can remain soft on the outside. The gentler someone is, the deeper their confidence is in themselves to handle anything that comes their way. Softness doesn't break, as it can bend and morph, but hardness does.

Another trait that is seen as feminine, and therefore weak, is the ability to remain receptive and surrender. To remain receptive and surrender is strength and takes deep inner trust to be able to go with the flow without fear and without wanting to control. Desire to control comes from fear.

Both masculine and feminine traits are necessary to be a whole person. There is a time for both. There is a time to be still and there is a time for action. To neglect one or the other creates imbalance.

Today, the feminine qualities need to be exalted. The feminine is as valuable and essential as the masculine. By ignoring and suppressing the feminine, the yin has been negatively impacted. Women need to be raised up to the same level of respect as men, so that the yin and yang are harmonious again. There will be a day when a man likened to a woman is no longer an insult, and that will be a day of balance between the yin and yang.

Chapter Four

TO LEAD
MUST FOLLOW

In the previous chapter we discussed the imbalance between the perceived value of the feminine and masculine. In this chapter we will continue this discussion by illustrating how valuable the feminine is, and, in fact, how imperative it is that it gains more power and equality in the eyes of society.

As you have noticed, this chapter's title is "to lead must follow," a line from the Grateful Dead. This statement expresses wisdom and deep truth. A good leader is acting upon the needs and desires of their followers. They are not acting upon their own wishes and desires. "To lead must follow" encapsulates this idea. A good leader hears what their followers need, then they act upon that. Action based in reception is strong leadership and is yin/yang working together in harmony.

Receptivity, when talking about archetypes, is deemed feminine and action is deemed masculine. A good leader would have equal amounts of feminine and masculine. If the leader took action without listening to the needs of their followers, then that action could be needless, destructive and perhaps occurring due to their own interest in power. The feminine is necessary for good leadership.

An ideal leader would have ample amounts of feminine qualities. They would have the capacity and willingness to listen, the empathy and compassion to care, and the humbleness to work with others cooperatively. Since a leader is acting on behalf of their followers, these are all necessary traits to have.

A leader who is denying their own feminine attributes risks being power-hungry, selfish, and acting independently from their followers' needs.

Due to the fact that this culture is masculine-dominated, those in power tend toward the masculine. Even women, when they achieve power and leadership positions, have historically tended toward the masculine. This is understandable, because the belief, albeit wrong, is that the masculine is superior and more powerful. Yet, as we have ascertained, the feminine is much needed in leadership positions. For a healthier cultural and environmental landscape, the feminine is exactly what is needed for harmonious and effective leadership.

Chapter Five

NOT ALL MEN

Not all men, but all women. All women have been affected by dangerous men. Even if a woman hasn't been physically or sexually assaulted, she has had to modify her behavior in order to feel safe, be it not going out at night by herself, or not traveling alone. Since all women are impacted, something needs to change.

Unfortunately, there is a statement being used in attempts to derail the progress for women. This statement is "not all men." "Not all men" is not only irrelevant, but it also tries to dismiss a movement that aims to protect women from harm. Even if these dangerous men only account for 10-20 percent of the male population, it is at a number where every woman knows a female friend that has been assaulted, if not herself. Since this is the case, the "not all men" statement is completely irrelevant to the reality of the issue being addressed by these movements aimed to protect women.

To help clarify by using an analogy, let's say there's a beach. There are one hundred sharks in the water at this beach. You are told that eighty of the sharks are harmless to humans, and twenty are Great Whites. Do you feel safe going in the water? Someone says, but "not all sharks" in the water are dangerous. Does this change your feeling of concern and safety? Are you now feeling like it's safe to go in the water? Or is that statement irrelevant, because the only relevant fact is that there are twenty dangerous sharks in the water. Even one in the water would make anyone not swim at that beach.

The "not all men" statement is as irrelevant as the "not all sharks" statement. It does not address the issue nor the reason for concern. Instead, it is a distraction and is, in fact, harmful to a movement aimed at protecting those in harm's way.

The women's movement is not trying to attack all men. If anything, it is asking for men's support. It is asking men to hold themselves and each other accountable for their actions and to call each other out. It seems that men are aware that it's not always safe for women, as they give certain safety advice to their daughters that they do not give to their sons. This illustrates that there is an awareness by men of the need for the movement, and luckily now there is an opportunity for them to help create a safer place for women.

Women deserve to feel safe. Women deserve to feel at ease walking down the street without the fear of men. Women deserve to feel safe going places alone without the fear of harassment. Women deserve to feel as safe as men do. Currently, our culture is allowing for men's misbehavior at the expense of the other fifty percent of the population. It is time for women to be as cared for by our society as men have been.

There is inequality occurring, and movements that are holding men accountable for their atrocities are paving the way for true equality, and therefore harmony. These movements are creating a safer world for women. All women.

Chapter Six

IT'S NOT BIOLOGY

Sitting in Introduction to Cultural Anthropology class at a public four-year university, we learned that males were biologically wired to spread their seed, so to speak. This was said with authority to a group of impressionable 18- to 21-year-olds. The basis of authority came from evolutionary biological theories. What was not mentioned, is that men have historically dominated anthropological studies, thereby focusing mostly on men's wiring and ignoring evolutionary biological traits women have that could have parallel implications.

There have been a lot of books published recently that debunk much of what we had been traditionally taught about men and women's sexuality, and this is most likely due to women getting into anthropological fields.

Unfortunately, our culture still rests on these outdated theories that excuse poor male behavior, labeling it as biological. This includes cheating on their partner and ogling women. Believing something to be biological not only excuses the behavior, but it also makes it seem inevitable and not something one can change about themselves.

The good news is that it's not biology causing poor male behavior towards women; it is taught through socialization.

The watering of the seed starts so young that it may seem biological, but it is not.

One specific aspect of this will be discussed below: the male gaze. The male gaze harms women by creating an atmosphere where they are objectified, feeding the wrong belief that women exist for men's visual and sexual pleasure. We are all taught that men are "visual creatures" and that women are the "beautiful" sex, thereby excusing men's behavior of ogling and sexualizing women. This extends to the point where it is socially acceptable for a married man to look at and sexualize women. There are many phrases in our current culture that excuse and normalize this, such as, "I'm just looking at the menu, not ordering."

It is not biology that causes men to ogle women. This is taught behavior. There is a tribe of people in Africa where the men are the "beautiful" ones, adorning themselves to attract the women. This demonstrates that it is not biological or innate for women to be considered the beautiful ones and for men to be the gazers. This is taught through socialization and perpetuated by the media. Both men and women have the capacity to ogle; the difference is that in our culture, women are not taught to do so, while men are.

Unfortunately, what accompanies ogling is the underlying objectification that is occurring. Movies and television primarily present the male gaze, with women's body parts being zoomed in on, reducing them to objects instead of human beings. As objects, women's value is determined solely by how useful they are for men's desires, such as being young and fertile, rather than being seen as fully realized individuals with their own desires.

Women watch the same media as men, so they see themselves through the lens of the male gaze. They then internalize their own objectification, believing that their bodies are for men's pleasure, not their own.

It is important to discuss more thoroughly what objectification means. To view someone as an object is to view them as a thing. This is unhealthy and damaging, because a thing has no feelings of its own and can be used for one's own desires without empathy. This lack of empathy towards women is continued through constant reinforcement that women's bodies are to be sexualized and looked at. Contributing to this is men's denial of their own yin, for if they held empathy for themselves, they would also be able to feel empathy towards another.

This objectification is another reason for the imbalance of yin and yang. Objects are not equal to humans, reinforcing the belief that women, the feminine, and therefore yin, have less value. For men to understand that women are their equal, they must stop seeing women as objects. The first step is for men to recognize that this behavior is not rooted in biology, but rather a symptom of a deep cultural myth that says women are made for men's pleasure. This myth was created by men for men and is completely untrue. Just as men live for their own existence and purpose, so do women.

It is crucial that we begin to see that men's views and behaviors towards women are learned and not innate biology. This means that this behavior can change. It requires an unlearning which can either start from refusing to water the belief or from completely uprooting the belief itself through inner awareness, compassion and resolve. Not surprisingly, the stillness and compassion needed for this work require reconnection to one's own yin and feminine qualities. It can be done, but it will take work. The health and harmony to follow will be worth the effort.

Chapter Seven

HIERARCHY

$\mathscr{W}$e live in a world consumed by the idea of hierarchy. Hierarchy implies superiority, which infers dominance. Dominance means to not see each other as equals. This applies to men's feeling of superiority over women, as well as humans' feelings of superiority over animals and the land.

Humans have developed a belief that the land and animals are for us, rather than living with us. With this belief of superiority, imbalance is occurring. Instead of living side by side in harmony with nature, which requires reciprocity and stewardship, we are using up her resources. Instead of allowing nature to unfold and thrive, we are dominating and controlling, causing destruction to animals, each other, and our home, planet Earth.

To see animals as inferior to us means we are not understanding life. Life exists in all of us, and the common thread of consciousness resides in us all. Understanding this leads to understanding that we are truly united. Life can choose to exist in the form of a human or a wild animal—it's still life. It is the same. That is why truly, harming another is to harm oneself. We are not separate.

Animals exist for their own purpose: to live. Just like you and I. All life should be free to exist for themselves. Every being has a purpose, whether it's the bee to pollinate or the worm to aerate the soil. All creatures are the children of Mother Earth and have inherent value.

Nature knows how to balance herself, and every creature has a purpose in maintaining homeostasis, so by our excessive destruction we are throwing off the natural balance. We are using up the land and using the animals, creating a sick environment. This is apparent in our overfished waters, factory farms, and destruction of biodiversity through deforestation and pollution. Again, this is due to excess productivity and dominance (yang) and the oppression and repression of stillness and reception (yin).

Understanding that we are all connected is of utmost importance. As said before in similar words, destroying life destroys our own. May we understand more fully the concept of reciprocity, to give as much as we take, and to honor our home and fellow inhabitants. Our life depends on it.

Chapter Eight

ALIGNMENT

Alignment is when the mind, heart, and action are all working in agreement. This first requires a connection to one's heart. The heart holds compassion; therefore, in alignment, action is coming from a place of compassion, which is the understanding that all beings suffer and therefore deserve consideration.

Much of our connection with the heart has been lost. We are a culture that values the mind over the heart. In this, what has been forgotten is that the eyes of awareness rest in the heart. It is not coincidental that the heart holds both awareness and compassion. To be aware is to have compassion, and to have compassion is to be aware. Sensitivity to this awareness has generally been lost, as we are trained at a young age to desensitize, thereby numbing our innate intelligence of awareness and compassion.

This desensitization is a result of the excessive yang masculine culture, where one is labeled weak if one expresses sensitivity and softness. Instead of sensitivity (and therefore awareness) being valued and seen as a valuable trait, it is dismissed as a negative attribute. This attitude toward sensitivity trains young people to repress and disconnect from their feelings, and therefore their heart, true self, and inner wisdom. In Traditional Chinese Medicine the heart is the yin organ that feels all the emotions of the other organs. To cut off from feelings, is to cut off from the heart.

Because we have trained people to cut off from themselves by shaming them, our culture is disconnected. To be in alignment, one must be connected to one's heart. To align with self, one must misalign with normative culture. The philosopher Jiddu Krishnamurti says it well with this quote: "It is no measure of health to be well-adjusted to a profoundly sick society."

It is easier to flow with mainstream society, as it takes strength and willpower to step out of that wavelength into nature's true flow. Meditation and spending time outside with trees and animals support the reunion with self, and therefore all nature. Through the stillness and quiet, one becomes open to the awareness within the heart. This is a receptive act of listening and allows for the heart to guide the mind, leading to correct action. Integrity is action in alignment. If one continues to only operate from the mental intellect, then it is only imbalanced action that will occur. The mind (yang) needs to connect with the deeper intellect of the heart (yin). For correct action, decisions need to be made by the heart via the mind. Yin and yang working together create balance, wholeness, and harmony.

Chapter Nine
CONCLUSION

$\mathscr{T}$he yin/yang symbol holds equal amounts of yin and yang. Equality is harmony. The yin has been excluded from decision-making and consideration for a very long time, and as it is being repressed in the individual it is repressed collectively in society. We are moving through life on one leg instead of two. We need equal amounts of both yin and yang to stand upright and move forward in wellness. This forgotten half is why we are in both environmental and social crises.

It comes down to the simple fact that

we overvalue yang and undervalue yin. It is time to ask ourselves and one another, why is it that we value dominance and competition over compassion and cooperation? Why does power need to be about how one can control and destroy another and not about stewardship and caretaking? Why do we disvalue anything related to women, the feminine, and yin? By doing so, we are not recognizing 50 percent of what makes up life. Let's start making it a norm to build each other and this world up, instead of using it up and breaking it down.

May we be grateful for what we have received in this lifetime and love, nourish, and protect it.

Nature speaks. May we listen.

www.ingramcontent.com/pod-product-compliance
Lightning Source LLC
Chambersburg PA
CBHW030030290326
41934CB00005B/560